Coun

FROM MANOR HOUSE TO STATELY HOME

Peter Brimacombe

The quintessential Englishman, Noel Coward, conceived the expression 'the stately homes of England' in a witty song written in 1938, around the time of Evelyn Waugh's vivid portrayal of aristocratic English life in his novel *Brideshead Revisited*. Today, stately homes such as Blenheim, Chatsworth and Longleat, together with smaller, yet equally stylish, country houses such as Ashdown, Antony and Tintinhull, provide a vivid insight into the nation's architectural, social, economic and cultural development, from the Middle Ages to the present day.

These magnificent houses were originally built to convey power, prestige, wealth and impeccable taste, places where privileged families lived in luxury and entertained lavishly, aided by hordes of servants whose wages were funded from rents paid by dutiful tenants. This was the good life on a grand scale; but times change and those halcyon days have long since gone.

Yet thankfully these great houses still survive, often due to The National Trust and English Heritage who immaculately preserve historic buildings which otherwise might have crumbled. A surprisingly large number of beautiful stately homes remain in private hands, however, and are carried into the 21st century by the love, dedication and ingenuity of their owners as an essential part of the nation's heritage.

Out of the Castle

The Medieval Manor House

Medieval manor houses began to appear in the English countryside as the need for secure fortresses gradually diminished, and the desire for more comfortable surroundings grew. A degree of caution still persisted, however, and places such as Baddesley Clinton and Ightham Mote retained both moat and gatehouse and, like Cotehele and Haddon Hall, faced into an easily defensible central courtyard.

Yet all of these manor houses were far more home than fortress, with all the latest comforts. Penshurst Place even had glass in its windows by the mid 14th century! Nevertheless, by modern standards these medieval houses were extremely spartan. Floors were beaten earth, hardened with clay mixed with ox blood, and covered with rushes. Interior walls downstairs were given a simple limewash, while those upstairs were merely boarded with plain wooden planks. Sanitation was exceedingly basic – personal hygiene was not considered important in those days.

The focal point of the medieval house was the great hall, which invariably featured a spectacularly high arch-braced timber roof – Cotehele and Penshurst are excellent examples. Here, the lord of the manor dined with his family at a refectory table, usually made from oak. It was positioned on a raised dais, and the retainers sat below at trestle tables, which could easily be removed to make way for dancing or for the servants to sleep on the floor. After dinner, the tops of the tables could be reversed to provide a clean surface for the daytime – hence the expression 'turning the tables'. When they became particularly dirty, they would be dismantled and swilled down outside. Penshurst Place retains two 6m (20ft) long trestle tables, said to be the only remaining examples of their kind in England.

ABOVE: *Cotehele is located in the picturesque Tamar Valley on the border of Devon and Cornwall. The gatehouse was built by Sir Richard Edgecumbe, who later fought alongside Henry Tudor at the Battle of Bosworth in 1485.*

LEFT: *Henry VIII was once entertained in the Baron's Hall of Penshurst Place in Sussex by the 3rd Duke of Buckingham. The King took such a liking to the house that he beheaded the owner and seized the property for himself.*

BELOW: *The Banqueting Hall in Haddon Hall, Derbyshire. Both the refectory table and the tapestry that hangs behind it date from the 15th century. The tapestry was reputedly given to the owner, Sir Henry Vernon, by King Henry VIII.*

ABOVE: *This 15th-century picture vividly portrays a medieval banquet complete with minstrels, whose function was to announce important guests and entertain the diners as they feasted.*

RIGHT: *The chapel at Lytes Cary in Somerset was constructed by Peter Lyte c.1343. The Lyte family lived here for more than 500 years and Peter Lyte's grandson is said to have been in Henry V's army at Agincourt.*

Behind the dais there was often a bay window, and some houses, such as the late 15th-century Great Chalfield Manor, had a window projecting from the first floor, known as an oriel. Most windows in medieval houses were deeply mullioned, with small, leaded glass panels.

Guests were entertained in the great hall, which often had a minstrel's gallery. In the centre of the hall there was usually an open fire blazing, its smoke escaping through a vent in the roof. A screen separated the hall from a primitive kitchen, pantry and buttery. Haddon Hall retains a fine example of a medieval kitchen, complete with 14th-century chopping boards and salting troughs for preserving meat. The kitchen was an all-male domain, a prized working place providing abundant warmth and free food – both of which were highly desirable in medieval England.

On the upper floor, the solar provided both sleeping accommodation and a refuge for the ladies to retire to if the evening's entertainment in the great hall became too boisterous; but a small window, called a squint, enabled them to keep a watchful eye on their menfolk. Houses such as Cotehele, Lytes Cary and Haddon Hall also had chapels for those occasions when the mood changed from pleasure to piety.

By present-day standards, life in the medieval manor would appear to have been somewhat basic; nevertheless, it represented a radical improvement on a cold, damp castle.

LEFT: *This medieval oriel window on the south front of Lacock Abbey in Wiltshire later became the subject of the earliest existing photographic negative, taken by William Fox Talbot in 1835.*

Medieval Craftsmen

Medieval craftsmen were able to work completely uninterrupted by architects, quantity surveyors, building inspectors or planning officers. Thus they were free to embellish basic building structures in a totally uninhibited personal style, conceiving exquisite artistry in paint, wood, metal and most particularly in stone.

A medieval stone carving from Buckland Abbey in South Devon.

Built to Impress

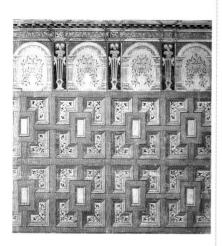

ABOVE: *An early 17th-century painted plaster wall with 'strapwork' design at Christchurch Mansion in East Anglia. This diamond-patterned red-brick Tudor house was built c.1548 for Edmund Withypoll, Lord of the Manor at Christchurch.*

Tudor & Jacobean Country Houses

The Middle Ages drew to a close when Henry Tudor's victory at Bosworth in 1485 finally ended the long-running Wars of the Roses. An age of peace and prosperity followed, and country houses began to develop far beyond their original functional purpose, to become the ultimate status symbol. Houses like Longleat, Burghley and Hardwick Hall were enormous compared with previous domestic buildings, and highly impressive. The owners were invariably self-made people wishing to flaunt their new-found wealth, and often built their houses on a hill – not in order to take advantage of the view, but so that they could easily be seen by their neighbours and by impressionable travellers.

Brick had become a favoured building material, used at places such as Hatfield House, Burton Constable and Burton Agnes Hall. Glass glittered in vast windows. Gables predominated, often gracefully curved as at Blickling, Montacute, Christchurch Mansion and the small yet exquisite Trerice, deep in the Cornish countryside. Everywhere, tall chimneys ensured that the smoke-filled great hall was a thing of the past.

Inside, floors were now constructed in brick, tile or stone flags; walls were covered with elaborately carved panelling; and ceilings were plastered, then lavishly decorated. The owner and his family had moved their sleeping quarters upstairs in search of greater privacy, so dramatic staircases were built to enable them to make grand entrances before their assembled guests. Although the water closet had replaced the primitive outdoor privy, there were still problems with hygiene. In Queen Elizabeth I's bedroom at Burghley, the curtains around the four-poster bed do not touch the ground, to prevent rats from climbing up and joining the occupant – an unnecessary precaution in this instance, as this famous monarch never actually slept there.

BELOW: *The Green Bedchamber at Hardwick Hall in Derbyshire, once the home of Bess of Hardwick. Much of the furniture and many tapestries at Hardwick, including those in the Green Bedchamber, are original 16th-century.*

ABOVE: *The tall, elaborate, brick chimneys at Hampton Court Palace. Built for Cardinal Wolsey, the palace fell into the hands of King Henry VIII following the disgrace of his once all-powerful minister.*

BELOW LEFT: *A painting of Burton Constable, in the East Riding of Yorkshire, towards the end of the 17th century. Sir John Constable had enlarged the original medieval house about a hundred years earlier. The Constable family still lives in the house.*

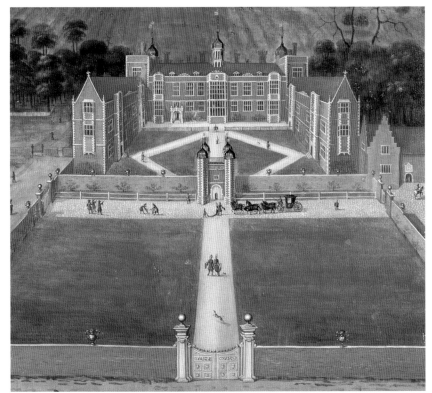

ABOVE: *Longleat in Wiltshire is widely considered to be the nation's finest English Renaissance house. Currently occupied by the Marquess of Bath, Longleat has been the family home for more than 450 years.*

A prime objective of Elizabeth's more ambitious courtiers was to achieve the ultimate accolade of entertaining the Queen in their home, although this could prove to be a costly business. Most great country houses of the day displayed a large, imposing portrait of Elizabeth I by leading artists such as Nicholas Hilliard, Marcus Gheeraerts or George Gower. Today these can be found in houses like Burghley, Hatfield and Hardwick Hall.

Architects such as Robert Smythson and Robert Lyminge planned and supervised construction, replacing the master mason. Smythson created Longleat and Hardwick, while Lyminge built Blickling and Hatfield. The latter was owned by Robert Cecil, the all-powerful minister for both Elizabeth and James I. By this time, ministers even had the temerity to attempt to upstage the monarch. Thomas Howard, 1st Earl of Suffolk and Lord Treasurer between 1605 and

1614, built Audley End, one of England's greatest Jacobean houses. 'Too large for a king,' sniffed King James, 'might do for a Lord Treasurer.' Not surprisingly, Howard was discovered to be guilty of embezzlement and completely disgraced.

Quite often, great houses in Tudor and Jacobean England were financed by unorthodox or questionable actions. Burghley was built using money acquired by Queen Elizabeth's Lord Treasurer while he was also Master of the Rolls. Drake purchased Buckland Abbey after capturing a Spanish galleon full of treasure, at a time when peace existed between England and Spain. Bess of Hardwick rose from humble origins via four husbands – who were progressively richer – to create Hardwick Hall.

This was an age of opulence, exuberance and extravagance, fully reflected in the architecture of the time. The stately home had well and truly arrived.

LEFT: *The Throckmorton coat of arms in the Tower Room at Coughton Court in Warwickshire. Much of the present house was originated in the early 16th century by Sir George Throckmorton, whose granddaughter married Sir Walter Raleigh.*

ABOVE: *The Great Hall at Audley End, a superb Jacobean mansion in Esssex, has the enormous proportions of a house conceived on a palatial scale c.1610 for the 1st Earl of Suffolk.*

The Clerical Connection

The development of the large-scale English country home in the 16th century was greatly helped by the Dissolution of the Monasteries. Land and building materials suddenly became available for secular purposes, and considerable numbers of skilled craftsmen, hitherto employed by the clergy, were forced to seek alternative work. Anglesey, Buckland and Lacock Abbies are converted monasteries, while Woburn Abbey and Wilton House were constructed on former monastic sites and Sudeley Castle was greatly extended utilising stone from Winchcombe Abbey.

Anglesey Abbey, near Cambridge.

Becoming Classical

The late 17th & early 18th-century

nigo Jones was a disciple of the Italian Andrea Palladio, creator of so many stylish palazzos in the Venetian Republic during the mid-16th century. In the 1640s, Jones remodelled the south front at Wilton House, the Earl of Pembroke's Wiltshire residence, bringing the first sighting of Palladianism to the English countryside. Sadly, his efforts were curtailed by the Civil War, and it was some time before this theme returned to England.

Shortly after the Restoration, an enchanting country house appeared high up on the Berkshire Downs – an exquisite, life-sized dolls' house, which seems to have been transported from Amsterdam. Created by the Dutchman William Winde, Ashdown is neat, refined and clean-cut, its elegant façade topped with hipped roof and jaunty cupola – a definitive country house, which set the architectural agenda for the next half-century. This was a marvellous period of English domestic building, when Vanbrugh created Castle Howard and Blenheim, while Talman remodelled Chatsworth; nevertheless, it is the smaller country houses such as Ashdown, Dyrham Park or Antony that truly capture the spirit of

BELOW: *The saloon at Blenheim Palace in Oxfordshire features murals and painted ceilings by Louis Laguerre. A superb silver centrepiece depicts the 1st Duke of Marlborough after his victory at the Battle of Blenheim on 17 August 1704.*

the age. All provided an ideal setting for the agreeable round of hunting and house-parties that characterised wealthy country living.

This era – known as the English baroque – produced more sophisticated, more understated, less ostentatious architecture than the preceding Tudor and Jacobean period. The contrast can best be appreciated at Hampton Court, where Wolsey's sprawling Tudor palace sits alongside Sir Christopher Wren's graceful extension, fashioned for King William III towards the end of the 17th century. The simply proportioned façade, with its classical columns and flat roof concealed behind a parapet, is echoed at Chatsworth and the East Front of Dyrham Park, both the work of William Talman, a rival of Wren. Sash windows generally succeeded the casement by the end of the 17th century, hipped roofs replaced gables, and lofty pairs of symmetrically placed chimneys appeared – all essentially Dutch characteristics. William Winde, Vanbrugh and Talman were all from Holland – but then so was the King.

ABOVE: *Ashdown House in Berkshire, created around 1663 for William, 1st Lord Craven, one of the wealthiest men of the period. Ashdown's formal box-and-gravel parterre is based on a 17th-century engraving.*

LEFT: *Vanbrugh's two parallel passages run the entire length of Castle Howard in Yorkshire. The Antique Passage houses the 4th Duke's marble busts, statues and urns, mainly collected on his Grand Tour of Europe in 1738. Castle Howard provided the setting for the enormously popular television adaptation of Evelyn Waugh's novel* Brideshead Revisited.

ABOVE: *Marcellus Laroon's painting c.1725 of a banquet conveys early 18th-century aristocratic life. Ladies gossip, gentlemen chat to pretty companions or pour generous amounts of wine, while a smug parson looks on and a dog begs for scraps.*

This was the age of the big-name architects, including Hawksmoor (who assisted Vanbrugh at both Castle Howard and Blenheim), Webb, Pratt and James Gibbs. Gibbs is thought to have worked at Antony, yet like Wren he was so involved with public works that he had precious little time for private houses. All these men were thoroughly knowledgeable both in construction techniques and the theory of design, and were familiar with the work of continental architectural

Grinling Gibbons

Grinling Gibbons was one of a number of outstanding craftsmen in the late 17th and early 18th centuries. Originally from Holland, Gibbons worked in both wood and stone, becoming Master Carver to King George I. His genius can be seen at St Paul's Cathedral, the Chelsea Hospital and in aristocratic homes such as Petworth, Burghley, Lyme Park, Chatsworth and Blenheim, where his jingoistic stone statuary depicts British lions savaging French fighting cocks.

The oak-panelled saloon at Lyme Park in Cheshire.

greats such as Palladio, Serlio, Bernini and Mansard – Wren had met the latter pair in Paris in 1665. Conversely, Vanbrugh was a talented amateur, and Castle Howard was his first ever building. Fortunately, he had the thoroughly professional Hawksmoor to guide him, and was subsequently preferred to Wren at Blenheim Palace.

As this period had an abundance of gifted master craftsmen, simple exteriors could conceal surprisingly sumptuous interiors. Men such as Grinling Gibbons, Tijou, Laguerre, Thornhill and Verrio conceived brilliant work, such as Thornhill's painted ceiling in the hall at Blenheim, or Antonio Verrio's dramatic Heaven Room and Hell Staircase at Burghley, considered his greatest masterpieces. Elsewhere, Verrio's work was less appreciated, being subsequently covered in flock wallpaper in Queen Anne's drawing room at Hampton Court. Different generations display different tastes, yet the English baroque was truly sublime.

ABOVE: *The doorway of the west front of Tintinhull in Somerset was constructed around 1722. Built of local honey-coloured Ham stone, the house looks particularly appealing in the late afternoon sun.*

LEFT: *The Heaven Room at Burghley in Lincolnshire features Antonio Verrio's dazzling portrayal of scenes from ancient mythology. These are so skilfully executed that the painted figures appear to be three-dimensional until approached and touched.*

The Golden Age

Great Georgian Houses

he 18th century represented the heyday of the English aristocracy and wealthy country gentry – more than two dozen peers owned lands extending to over 100,000 acres. It was a period that witnessed the full flowering of English domestic architecture. Hugely rich and cultured owners engaged talented architects such as William Kent, Colen Campbell, John Carr and Robert Adam to design their dream houses, before filling them with furniture by Chippendale, Sheraton and Hepplewhite, and paintings acquired on the Grand Tour of Europe. These houses would subsequently be surrounded with parks newly land-scaped by Capability Brown, at that time considered the height of fashion and good taste in the great outdoors.

The era began with the reintroduc-tion of Palladianism, largely by Kent, who had travelled and studied exten-sively in Italy. He worked at Badmin-ton, Rousham, Holkham Hall and Houghton Hall, as well as at Horse Guards' Parade in London.

Houghton Hall was the country seat of Sir Robert Walpole, England's first ever Prime Minister. The cost of construction was so exorbitant that Sir Robert destroyed all the bills in order to conceal precisely how much he had lavished – out of public funds – on this house in Norfolk, now widely regarded as one of the nation's finest examples of Palladian architecture.

Critics consider Palladianism to be far too severe, and believe that rigid adherance to geometric principles and slavish imitation of Palladio completely stifles individual creativity. It was the view held by Robert Adam, and this good-looking, talented, fiercely ambitious young Scot almost single-handedly swept away Palladianism to establish his own highly personal neo-classical style, which was to dominate England for the rest of the century. 'Mr Adam produced a total change in the architecture of this country,' stated his obituary in the *Gentleman's Magazine* of 1792.

ABOVE: *The Yellow Drawing Room at Harewood House in Yorkshire is an outstanding example of the genius of Robert Adam. The star-and-circle motif in the carpet echoes the pattern of the ceiling. The two large, ornate mirrors are by Thomas Chippendale.*

LEFT: *The powerful Whig politician and England's first Prime Minister, Sir Robert Walpole, was the original owner of Houghton Hall, where he entertained on a grand scale.*

LEFT: *The Gallery at Hagley Hall, Worcestershire, Viscount Cobham's West Midland seat, runs the entire length of the east front. Its paintings and sculptures were damaged in the 19th century when the family used the gallery as an indoor cricket pitch.*

BELOW: *The aptly-named Red Bedroom at Sledmere in the Yorkshire Wolds, today owned by the 8th Baronet Sir Tatton Sykes. The 4th Baronet, a horse-racing fanatic, travelled every year on horseback from Sledmere to Epsom to attend the Derby.*

The evolution of Georgian architecture was driven as much by new building regulations as by pure aesthetic considerations. Remembering the Great Fire of London, Parliament had passed a series of acts in the early 18th century in order to reduce fire risk. Thus, recessed window frames, the disappearance of wooden eaves, stone parapets to replace wooden cornices, and the introduction of wrought-iron railings, balconies and lamp holders all stemmed from legislation rather than artistic activity.

Adam's real genius lay in his ability as an interior designer, effortlessly setting a dazzling stage where high society could perform – reception rooms for sparkling conversation and witty repartee, as ladies paraded the latest fashions; dining rooms where gentlemen sat for many hours after dinner, consuming vast quantities of port while settling affairs of state; ballrooms for grand occasions, and boudoirs for romantic assignations. This was the world that Jane Austen described so well – civilised, urbane, refined; country chic by candlelight.

The proud owner could summon Turner to paint his property, as did the 2nd Earl at Harewood or the 3rd Earl of Egremont at Petworth. Stubbs or Morland might portray his horse and other animals, Sir Joshua Reynolds or Thomas Gainsborough his family. As Reynolds was painting the 4th Duke of Marlborough at Blenheim Palace, the eminent artist accidentally dropped snuff on the carpet. The Duchess

Thomas Chippendale

Thomas Chippendale was born in 1718 in Otley, Yorkshire, not far from Harewood House, where he was responsible for much of the furniture and furnishings, including picture frames, fire screens, mirrors, bookcases, library steps and even commodes. Working mainly in mahogany, Chippendale raised the standard of English furniture design to challenge continental Europe. The example pictured right is from Newby Hall in North Yorkshire.

summoned a footman to sweep it up. 'Go away,' said Reynolds, august first president of the Royal Academy, 'the dust you make will do more harm to my painting than my snuff to the carpet.' Such was life in an English stately home during the 18th century.

ABOVE: *Bowood, the Wiltshire home of the Marquis of Lansdowne, is a fine Georgian property designed by Henry Keene and Robert Adam. It is beautifully set in an exquisite landscaped park designed by Capability Brown.*

LEFT: *The elaborately carved and painted woodwork in the Chinese Room of Claydon House in Buckinghamshire is by Luke Lightfoot. The furniture was made in Canton around 1800.*

End of an Era

Fine Regency Houses

The Regency period, in architectural terms, is generally considered to have begun with Robert Adam's death in 1792, and continued for almost forty years, to encompass both the rule of the flamboyant Prince Regent and his subsequent inauspicious reign as George IV. The dominant architect was John Nash, fortunate in having as his patron this earlier Prince of Wales with a passion for architecture. Nash's wife was rumoured to be one of the Prince Regent's many mistresses.

The architecture of the period was eclectic and reflected the mood of these fun-loving years – Greek revival mixed with neo-Gothic, plus a dash of eastern influence at Sezincote in the Cotswolds, designed by S.P. Cockerell, and at the Royal Pavilion in Brighton. This striking seaside oriental extravaganza was originally proposed by Humphrey Repton, but it was Nash who took credit for it.

Nash, ever an architectural opportunist, became the star attraction, while Repton, Soane, Smirke, the Burtons and Cockerell played only

BELOW: *Belvoir Castle in Leicestershire is the ancestral home of the Dukes of Rutland. There are superb examples of Regency furniture and decor in the Elizabethan Saloon, the Grand Dining Room and the Regent's Gallery.*

minor roles. Some of these assisted Nash with his visionary development of terraced town houses around the vast urban oasis of Regents Park.

The Regency period is invariably associated with Nash's complete transformation of central London; nevertheless, a number of impressive houses were created in the countryside. Among these were Belvoir Castle, a neo-Gothic fantasy conceived by the 5th Duke of Rutland's chaplain following a disastrous fire in 1816; Tatton Park, once owned by the eccentric Lord Egerton, an ideal place to study Regency furniture and furnishings, and Smirke's Normanby Hall.

Cast-iron technology achieved new heights in the early 19th century, adjacent to Doric doorways and porches. The use of stucco became widespread; verandas, balconies and enlarged bay and bow windows predominated. Regency architecture represented an interim stage between Adam's refined elegance and the Victorian grandeur that followed.

ABOVE: *The Brighton Pavilion started life as a simple seaside cottage for the Prince Regent, but before long it was extended by John Nash into its present extravagant form.*

LEFT: *The furniture and decor of the Music Room at Tatton Park in Cheshire typify prevailing taste in the Regency period.*

LEFT: *In 1815 Sir Robert Smirke, architect of the British Museum, was commissioned by Sir Robert Sheffield to remodel Normanby Hall in Lincolnshire.*

19

Let There be Light

The Victorian Country House

In Queen Victoria's reign, the British Empire covered more than one quarter of the globe. The ruling class was affluent, assertive and supremely self-confident – characteristics that were reflected in the grandeur of homes influenced equally by the Gothic revival and by radical advances in technology. The Victorians loved the past, yet wanted their creature comforts. In came electricity, hot and cold running water, better cooking facilities and greatly improved sanitation, all installed within buildings festooned with towers, turrets and elaborately carved stonework – medievalist, but with all mod cons!

ABOVE: *The Victorian High Gothic chimney piece in Crace's State Drawing Room at Knebworth in Hertfordshire displays the Lytton family crest. Edward Bulwer-Lytton inherited the house in 1843 and transformed it into a neo-Gothic fantasy.*

RIGHT: *Highclere in Berkshire was transformed from a simple Georgian mansion by Sir Charles Barry for Henry Herbert, 3rd Earl of Carnarvon, shortly after the young Victoria had inherited the throne in 1837.*

It was an age of opulence. Outside, there was stucco, decorated chimney pots and the re-appearance of half-timbering. Inside were elaborate fireplaces and chimneypieces, intricate cast-iron balustrades and ornate plasterwork – the Victorians were definitely not minimalist! The cholera epidemic of 1848 laid new emphasis on the need for effective plumbing and drainage, and efficiently piped water led to a proliferation of basins, baths and water closets. Victorian society was extremely pious, and cleanliness certainly came next to godliness!

A rapidly growing railway network considerably improved access to country houses, where butlers, sometimes more lordly than their masters, commanded an army of staff – deferential footmen and valets, housekeepers, formidable cooks and pretty young chambermaids. In the grounds, coachmen, grooms, gardeners and gamekeepers abounded on large estates.

ABOVE: *The Gallery at Holker Hall, the Cumbrian home of Lord and Lady Cavendish, represents a Victorian update of galleries found in the great Elizabethan houses. The new wing at Holker replaced part of the house destroyed by fire in 1871.*

Spearheading the Gothic revival were architects such as Sir Charles Barry, Norman Shaw and the splendidly named Augustus Welby Northmore Pugin. Pugin led the neo-medieval movement that swept across the nation from Cragside in Northumberland, designed by Norman Shaw for the wealthy arms manufacturer William Armstrong, to Highclere in Berkshire, seat of the Earls of Carnarvon. Highclere's exterior resembles the House of Commons, also designed by Barry; the library reflects his Reform Club in London.

ABOVE: *This fine Victorian photograph portrays a group of servants from both the house and the estate. Many present-day owners take the opportunity to be photographed with their staff at the annual estate gathering.*

In the 4th Earl's day, Highclere represented the archetypal Victorian stately home, filled with a masculine air of power and affluence, from the grandiose Gothic Saloon to the Smoking Room, reeking with the smell of cigars, popularised by Prince Albert and the Prince of Wales. The Earl was a powerful Tory politician, a cabinet minister in Disraeli's government, and the Prime Minister was a frequent visitor to Highclere. Disraeli lived nearby at Hughenden Manor, purchased with money provided by wealthy Tory friends when he became leader of the party.

Not far from Hughenden lies Waddesdon Manor, built for Baron Ferdinand de Rothschild to resemble a fairytale French chateau. The Rothschilds were both extravagant and eccentric. At Tring, Lord Rothschild's cows were rumoured to munch out of silver troughs, while Alfred Rothschild's pony trap was pulled by zebras.

ABOVE: *'Summer life in this enchanting place … is really Paradise and I should be content always to live here,' wrote Queen Victoria in her journal on 26 May 1853 of Osborne, her private residence near Cowes on the Isle of Wight.*

RIGHT: *An elaborate lamp on the stairwell at Osborne, which also contains a life-size statue of Prince Albert, Victoria's Prince Consort. Albert was involved in all aspects of Osborne's design.*

William Morris

William Morris was a paradox. His wild, unruly hair, bushy beard and piercing eyes indicated the quintessential revolutionary socialist, artist and poet. In reality, Morris was born into a comfortable middle-class family, educated at Marlborough College and Oxford University, and made a good living designing and manufacturing conservative wallpapers, fabrics and furniture for privileged, wealthy customers.

The Queen took one look at the Royal Pavilion at Brighton after inheriting it, and was not amused. She promptly sold it to the local council and built her own seaside home on the Isle of Wight. Osborne House is not a mock medieval castle – Victoria already had several genuine ones – but an imposing Italianate villa created by her beloved Albert. Victoria was blissfully happy at Osborne, yet it was not to everyone's taste. Lord Roseberry, Prime Minister after Gladstone, said he believed the drawing room to be the ugliest in the world – until he saw Balmoral!

The English country house was at its zenith when in 1894 Parliament introduced death duties, which threatened its very future.

Style and Substance

The Edwardian Country House

The Edwardian era was witty, stylish and sophisticated – Sir Edward Lutyens declared, 'architecture is building with wit'. Lutyens began his eminent architectural career by designing a series of luxurious, rather traditional country houses for the newly successful captains of industry, replacing the nobility in desiring homes of quality and distinction – new money embracing old values in search of respectability. The ultimate example was Castle Drogo, built for Julius Drewe, who had amassed a fortune from a chain of grocery shops. This neo-medieval fortress was begun by Lutyens in 1910, as the first skyscrapers were appearing in New York.

BELOW: *Coleton Fishacre is set in a marvellous tropical garden on the south Devon coast. Its architect, Oswald Milne, was a follower of Lutyens, whose trademark mullioned windows, tall chimneys and steeply pitched roofs are seen here.*

Lutyens also converted a ruined Tudor fort on Holy Island into a comfortable residence for Thomas Hudson, founder and owner of *Country Life*, avidly read by the county set and by those eager to join. Lutyens was so dominant that it might be said he postponed the introduction of modern architecture into the nation for more than half a century, to the detriment of progressives like Charles Rennie Mackintosh.

ABOVE: *The Common Room at Goddards in Surrey typifies the relaxed sophistication of Lutyens, who enlarged the house in 1910. Built as a holiday home for impoverished ladies, Goddards is now maintained by the Landmark Trust.*

LEFT: *The Tea Room at Polesden Lacey in Surrey contains the French furniture favoured by its Edwardian owner, Mrs Ronald Greville. The room beautifully portrays the atmosphere of unhurried luxury that prevailed at the time.*

BELOW: *The portcullis in the entrance hall at Castle Drogo in Devon remains in full working order. Above, carved in the granite, is the Drewe lion and motto. The owner, Julius Drewe, died only a year after his new castle was completed.*

Country houses by architects such as Lutyens, Charles Voysey and Oswald Milne display impeccable taste, acute attention to detail, and a profound sense of the vernacular. Houses like Coleton Fishacre, built by Milne for Sir Rupert d'Oyly Carte and financed by hugely successful productions of Gilbert and Sullivan, blend neatly into the landscape. Asymmetrical façades, massive buttresses, long sloping roofs and rough-cast walls were Voysey's hallmarks. Lutyens also loved generous roofs, tall chimney stacks, mellow bricks and exposed woodwork. The accent in the Edwardian country home was on convenience and comfort. Their owners were fastidious rather than flamboyant, establishing a trend that lasted through the First World War and beyond.

Towards Tomorrow

Modern Times

At one time, aspiring owners commissioned contemporary architects to create all the latest trends, but this concept ceased after the Second World War. Today, cutting-edge architects such as Foster, Rogers and Grimshaw are largely ignored in favour of designers like Quinlan Terry. A favourite of the Prince of Wales, Terry creates neo-Palladian houses, which are tasteful, yet hardly state-of-the-art.

It is an interesting paradox that the further the nation advances, the more reactionary English domestic building has become, unlike in America or Scandinavia. Thus, Westover Hall is neo-medieval, Wisley mock-Tudor, and Chartwell and Charleston fascinating purely for the way famous owners enhanced conventional dull buildings. Only a few places, such as the gloriously art deco Eltham Palace, portray modern times.

ABOVE: *Chartwell, overlooking the Kent Weald, was acquired by Winston Churchill in 1922. Over the next 40 years, Churchill transformed a rather unprepossessing Victorian house into a place redolent with atmosphere.*

RIGHT: *Stephen Courtauld, of the illustrious textile family, was responsible for the stunning art deco interior of Eltham Palace in south London in the 1930s. The dining room exemplifies this very striking period of design.*

A combination of rising costs and taxation have threatened the survival of the large-scale country home, but a rearguard action by organisations like The National Trust and English Heritage, essential for the preservation of the status quo, has saved the day. Individual owners have proved remarkably robust, financing enormous running costs by opening their houses to the public and introducing horse trials, craft fairs, corporate entertainment, usage as film sets, and outdoor concerts, both classical and rock. 'I suspect there is more interest in the filming than the house,' muses the Earl of Pembroke, whose family home at Wilton provided a sumptuous setting for *Sense & Sensibility* and *The Madness of King George*. 'Tina Turner paid for the renovation of the East Court Tympanum, Dire Straits for the Chambers Bridge,' declares the Marchioness of Tavistock at Woburn Abbey. Such ingenuity ensures that the great English stately home remains very much alive and well.

ABOVE: *Charleston lies in the lee of the South Downs in Sussex. For many years it was the home of Vanessa Bell, her husband Clive and her lover, the artist Duncan Grant, all members of the Bohemian Bloomsbury Set.*

LEFT: *Wisley in Surrey has been the headquarters of the Royal Horticultural Society since 1904. The house is built in mock-Tudor style, but using authentic Tudor timber-work. The pond was designed by Sir Geoffrey Jellicoe.*

Glossary

Baroque An expressive, extravagant and decorative style, dating from the 17th and 18th centuries.

Buttery A room for storing food and drink.

Casement A vertically hinged opening window.

Cornice A device used to stop water running down the face of an outside wall; decorative moulding between internal walls and ceiling.

Cupola A small domed structure positioned on top of a roof.

The central cupola at Sudbury Hall in Derbyshire.

Eaves The lower part of a roof which overhangs a wall.

Façade The front or principal face of a building.

Frieze A horizontal band of decoration.

A plaster frieze panel in the Great Hall at Montacute in Somerset.

Gable A triangular upper section of wall supporting a sloping roof.

Gothic A style of architecture developed in the Middle Ages.

Gothic revival The re-introduction of medieval concepts into the architecture of the 19th century.

Hipped roof Replaced gables at the end of the 17th century. The sides of the roof slope inward to the roofline.

Medieval A period of history dating from the Norman Conquest in 1066, ending with the Battle of Bosworth in 1485 and the start of the Tudor age.

Mortar A mixture of sand and lime, sometimes clay, used to bind stone or brickwork.

Mullion A vertical bar dividing the panes of a window.

Neo-classicism Architecture based on Greek and Roman principles.

Ogee A curved architectural form.

Ogeed windows at Lacock Abbey in Wiltshire.

Oriel A projecting window bracketed out from a wall.

Palladian A style of architecture derived from the 16th-century Italian architect, Andrea Palladio.

Pediment Formalised classical gable forming a shallow triangle on the front of a building.

Portico A colonnade or covered veranda in classical architecture.